Kailie!

Happy Birthday!!!

Hope you have an amazing Birthday and that the Jesus Horse carries you onward and upward!!

Love you long time!

♡ Emma

© 2013 Emma Latheron.

All Rights Reserved.

ISBN: 978-1-304-46917-5

Praise for Latheron's debut, *The Jesus Horse*:

"What colour is the sky in Emma's world?" – Doug Girling, hopeful t-shirt entrepreneur & film producer.

"BARK! (giggle) Barkbarkbark! Emma, you freak!" – Kimberly Lopez, respected literary critic / accountant.

"This is the best essay I've ever read in the world ever. Ever." – Kyla Girling, over-reactor, superfan & editor.

"Oprah's book club will be all over this! The world needs [these] stories!" – Aron Wilson, creative writing mentor & publicist.

"I am so inspired by reading this…thank you for shining a new light on my life" – Amber Gamache, religious leader / student.

"I won't lie—I peed myself a little laughing." – Ryan Pepplar, comedy guru and bladder control specialist.

"I don't get it."
– Sid Latheron, man half responsible for the genetic makeup of the author of *The Jesus Horse*.

The Jesus Horse

Written by Emma Latheron

Illustrated by Conor Watts

Edited by Kyla Girling

Editor's dedication:

October 5th, 2013

For my talented, lovely & hilarious friend Emma:

A special illustrated version of her "biology essay"

With special thanks to Conor Watts for his amazing

illustrations

&

Extra-special thanks to the Latheron family, for nurturing, feeding, sheltering, and laughing at *and* with the author for the past thirty years. You've done a marvellous job & we wouldn't have her any other way!

The Galapagos Tortoise, aka the Jesus Horse is the oldest living biblical figure, ever in history. Ever.

Jesus used to ride his horses through the desert so he could escape from the devil. Unfortunately, Jesus Horses are one of the slowest moving animals in existence, so sometimes the son of God was unable to escape the devil and was therefore tempted by Satan's trickery.

Another time, when Jesus was trying to lead the Jews out of Egypt, the only means of escape was to cross the desert; however, because the sand was so hot, it was burning their feet. Jesus improvised and got 400 of his fastest Jesus Horses—two for each Jew. With their belongings tied to their backs, the Jews held the reins of their horses and stood on their backs to ride through the desert. This is why it took forty days and forty nights to get through the unbearable desert.

Sometimes, when Jesus and his disciples had to fight the electrolytes, they had to sacrifice some tortoises for their mighty shells, which are made of pure sunshine dust. When God created these magnificent animals he fused together his two favourite things, sunshine dust and unicorn poop. Unicorn poop is now obviously very hard to get, as the unicorns went extinct during the historic war between God and Adam & Eve.

There is very little actually known about the Adam & Eve versus God war. Over the past millions of years, the story has been watered down so that the real truth of this war may never be revealed.

Recently a book was published, titled: *The Tempting Garden: Just How Tempting Was It?* This book was not easily or happily received; however, it was hard for people to deny just how tasty apples are, so, if we're honest, can we really blame Eve for eating one? No, we cannot. After all, apples are one of the staple foods in the Jesus Horse diet. When Eve was tempted by the apple on the tree - which was put there as a tester by the big guy upstairs - Eve first had a unicorn taste the apple to make sure it wasn't poisoned. That unicorn died immediately. But naïve Eve, (unknown fact: the word naïve originated with Eve) continued to eat the apple, because she thought she was better than everyone else (typical first-woman-on-earth syndrome).

God was obviously not pleased with Eve's behaviour, and, as a punishment, took all of the unicorns away from Adam and Eve and then kicked the pair of them out of Heaven. When the dust cleared, all that remained were Jesus Horses and ferrets. Ferrets were quickly dismissed as they are one of the worst animals ever created, which left plenty of room for Jesus Horses to flourish. And flourish they did! So much so, in fact, that they took over the whole of the Galapagos Islands.

The Galapagos Islands were first discovered by some douche named Charles Darwin. He tried to override God and name Jesus Horses "Galapagos Tortoises", but people were obviously not taking to that stupid name. So, Darwin was taken back to England, his homeland, and once there was tarred and feathered. People started to call him Galapagos Quack so that he would learn his lesson. Galapagos Quack later died of tar poisoning; apparently that stuff is pretty bad for the lungs.

Jesus Horses have been around for millions of years, but, unfortunately, due to the decreasing knowledge and interest in their origin, people are slowly forgetting just how amazing these animals are.

I hope that you will one day visit the Galapagos Islands to behold these amazing horses, and be sure to spread the good word about them for many generations to come—after all, you are blessed enough to be alive during the time of the Jesus Horse.

The End.

Emma Latheron currently resides in Vancouver, BC. She grew up in beautiful Tsawwassen, where she enjoys spending time with her family, including her nieces and her nephew, and the family dog Mika. She is an animal lover who especially loves dolphins. Many of her friends insist she is the funniest person they know. Emma's own personal deity is Oprah Winfrey, who she had the honour of meeting in person this past year. This is her first book; she is currently working on her second project, a non-fiction compilation with the working title *Where Did I Go Wrong?*